MARTIAL ARTS

KICKBOXING

Klaus Nonnemacher is a seven-time world champion in kickboxing, and he is currently vice president of the WKA. The models are Suzanne Grayson (orange belt), Christopher Pritchard (green belt), and Patrick Quinn (black belt gold bar).

Please visit our web site at: **www.garethstevens.com**
For a free color catalog describing Gareth Stevens Publishing's list of high-quality books and multimedia programs, call 1-800-542-2595 (USA) or 1-800-387-3178 (Canada). Gareth Stevens Publishing's fax: (414) 332-3567.

Library of Congress Cataloging-in-Publication Data

Nonnemacher, Klaus.
    Kickboxing / Klaus Nonnemacher. — North American ed.
        p. cm. — (Martial arts)
    Includes bibliographical references and index.
    ISBN 0-8368-4194-8 (lib. bdg.)
    1. Kickboxing—Juvenile literature. I. Title. II. Martial arts (Milwaukee, Wis.)
  GV1114.65.N66   2004
  796.815—dc22   2004045203

This North American edition first published in 2005 by
Gareth Stevens Publishing
A World Almanac Education Group Company
330 West Olive Street, Suite 100
Milwaukee, WI 53212 USA

Original edition © 2003 by David West Children's Books. First published in Great Britain in 2003 by Raintree, Halley Court, Jordan Hill, Oxford OX2 8EJ, part of Harcourt Education. Raintree is a registered trademark of Harcourt Education Ltd. This U.S. edition © 2005 by Gareth Stevens, Inc. Additional end matter © 2005 by Gareth Stevens, Inc.

Photographer: Sylvio Dokov
David West editor: James Pickering
David West designer: Gary Jeffrey
Gareth Stevens editor: Alan Wachtel
Gareth Stevens designer: Steve Schraenkler
Gareth Stevens art direction: Tammy West
Gareth Stevens production: Jessica Morris

Photo Credits:
Abbreviations: (t) top, (m) middle, (b) bottom, (r) right, (l) left, (c) center

All photos by Sylvio Dokov except Getty Images: 6(t); John Gichigi/Allsport 6(b), 11(tl), 13(br), 15(b), 18(tl), 25(b); Paula Bronstein/Liaison 22(tl). Klaus Nonnemacher: Michael Deubner 24(b), GES 21(tr).

Sylvio Dokov was born in Sofia, Bulgaria. For the past two decades, he has been one of Europe's leading martial arts photographers. Sylvio works from his own studio in Telford, Shropshire.

Printed in the United States of America

1 2 3 4 5 6 7 8 9 08 07 06 05 04

MARTIAL ARTS

KICKBOXING

Klaus Nonnemacher

GARETH**STEVENS**
GS
PUBLISHING
A World Almanac Education Group Company

CONTENTS

Introduction 5
History 6
Equipment 7
Kickboxing Basics 8
Jab 9
Right Cross 10
Uppercut 12
Hook 13
Front Kick 14
Roundhouse Kick 16
Side Kick 18
Low Kick 20
Knee Strike 22
Back Kick 24
Countering Punches 26
Countering Kicks 28
Useful Information 30
Kickboxing Terms 31
Index 32

INTRODUCTION

Martial arts are ways of learning to defend yourself and develop physical and mental discipline. Many of them are also international competitive sports. Experts agree that the only way to really learn a martial art is to train with a qualified teacher.

This book introduces some of the basic techniques of kickboxing, a popular martial art that combines karate and boxing. Read the text carefully and look closely at the pictures to see how to do some basic kickboxing moves.

HISTORY

Joe Lewis kicks a heavy bag in about 1963.

Traditional martial arts from the Far East, especially karate, became popular in the United States after World War II (1939–1945). At first, competitors in karate tournaments were not allowed to make full contact, because it was considered too dangerous. Soon, safety equipment was introduced to make full-contact karate matches possible. Full-contact karate evolved into modern kickboxing when competitors adopted training techniques from boxing to improve their fitness.

In 1974, American Joe Lewis became the first official world heavyweight kickboxing champion.

Kickboxing evolved from full-contact karate.

Competitors in full-contact karate wore long pants, and they used some techniques that were more closely related to karate than to boxing.

EQUIPMENT

Proper safety equipment is vital in modern kickboxing. Safety gear helps kickboxers avoid injury in training and competition. Boxing gloves and foot protectors safegaurd the hands and feet, as well the person receiving a punch or a kick. Without safety equipment, even a light blow can be very dangerous.

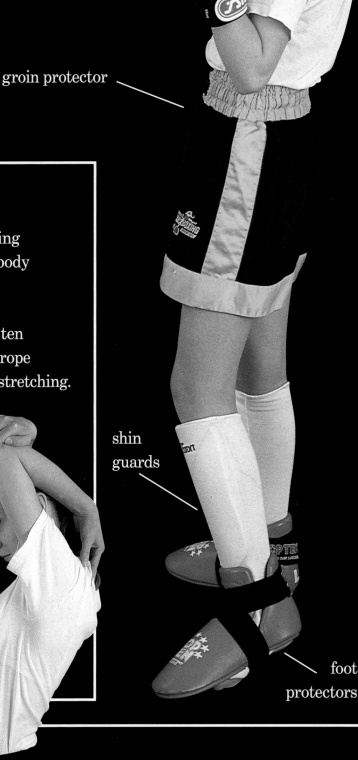

head guard

mouth guard

boxing gloves

groin protector

shin guards

foot protectors

WARMING UP

Before practicing kickboxing techniques, warm up the body to prevent injury.

Start by jumping rope for ten minutes. Follow jumping rope with ten minutes of light stretching.

Repeat the exercises pictured three times for fifteen seconds each. To avoid pulling a muscle, do not stretch too far. A proper stretch causes only a slight strain.

KICKBOXING BASICS

Before learning any basic kickboxing moves, all students must learn how to make a fist correctly and how to stand in the fighting stance.

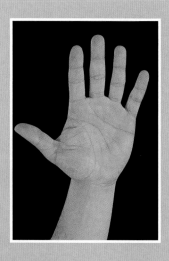  

Making a fist correctly helps prevent injuries. Open your hand flat, with your fingers apart. Fold your fingers tightly into your palm and bind your folded fingers with your thumb.

FIGHTING STANCE

Stand with your knees slightly bent, both feet pointing forward, elbows held close to your body, and fists raised. Lift the heel of the back foot slightly to allow for quick reactions. Keep the lower body turned slightly, offering only a narrow target area to an opponent. Lean the upper body slightly forward, holding your chin close to your chest. Protect your head with your shoulders and raised fists. From this basic combat position, you can perform every foot and fist technique in this book.

JAB

The jab is the most basic, and the most important, punch in kickboxing. Not only is it the quickest way to make contact with an opponent's head, but also it helps a kickboxer find the right distance from which to fight.

A jab can be thrown to the upper or lower part of an opponent's head.

The kickboxer on the right has dropped her protection and suffers a knockout.

1 **2** **3**

THE BASIC JAB

1. Stand in the fighting stance and focus on the opponent.

2. With your rear hand protecting your face, punch with your front hand, turning your hip and shoulder into the punch and shifting your weight onto the forward leg. At the moment the punch lands, turn the fist.

3. Immediately after making contact, pull the punching arm back for protection.

RIGHT CROSS

When a kickboxer is on the floor for ten seconds, the referee calls a knockout, and the fight is over. The right cross causes more knockouts than any other tactic.

1. Stand in a fighting stance, with the left foot forward and your weight on this foot. Focus on your opponent.

2. Extend the right arm from your shoulder to the opponent's head. Turn your fist as it lands on the opponent's face or body.

3. Shift your weight back to your right foot and bring your left arm up to protect your body and face.

1

2

3

Both boxers have dropped their protection, opening themselves up to cross punches.

The kickboxer on the right keeps his left arm up for protection as he delivers a right cross.

THAI PAD PRACTICE

Practicing with a handheld training pad, or thai pad, helps improve punching skills. As a partner moves around with the pad, try to find the right distance from which to punch. Start slowly, then try some quicker moves. If you feel confident, try a right cross.

UPPERCUT

The uppercut targets the small space between the defending hand and the chin. This technique is both powerful and dangerous.

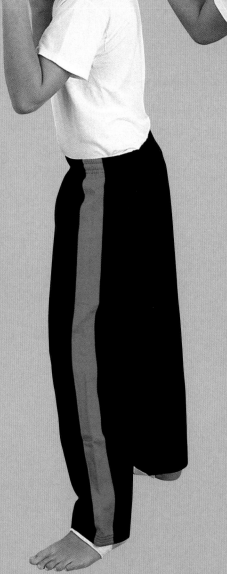

1

2

A successful uppercut gets its power from the thrust of the legs and back, as well as the arm.

1. Stand in a fighting stance, with your weight on the forward leg and your knees slightly bent. Focus on your opponent.

2. While throwing the punch, straighten the legs to create an upward flow of power through the knees, hips, and shoulders.

HOOK

The hook can be used for defense or attack. Throw a hook with the elbow away from the body. Because the hips and shoulders turn with the punch, the impact of the hook is very great.

1

2

3

1. Stand in a fighting stance.

2. Turn the forward leg and arm in a quarter circle.

3. Raise the forward heel and turn that whole side of the body into the punch. Use your rear arm to protect your face and the other side of your body.

A hook should be used at medium or close range.

When it is mastered, the hook is a very dangerous knockout technique.

FRONT KICK

The front kick is a fast technique that can be used either to stop an approaching opponent or to attack an opponent from a mid to a long range. Try to make contact with the ball of the foot, striking the opponent's face or stomach. The toes of the kicking foot should be pulled back to prevent injury.

1

2

1. Stand in a fighting stance and focus on the opponent. The feet should be almost in line with the shoulders, and the body should be turned to the right, leaning slightly forward.

2. Bring the rear knee to the front and raise the knee while turning the supporting leg to the side. Turn the rear arm and shoulder forward.

Thrusting the hip forward behind the kick will increase the front kick's power and reach.

3

3. Snap the raised leg forward while pulling your toes back, flexing the foot, and thrusting the hip forward. Try not to stretch the knee completely, because the power of the kick can injure the knee. It is important to snap the kicking leg back again before setting it down.

Accomplished kickboxers can throw a front kick to an opponent's head, but they must keep good balance at all times.

ROUNDHOUSE KICK

The roundhouse kick is a semicircular kick that can be used at different heights. This powerful kick hits with the top of the foot or with the shin.

A roundhouse kick can use the shin to make contact with an opponent's body or head.

1. Stand in a fighting stance and focus on your opponent. The left fist should be at about eye level, and the right fist should be at cheek level.

2. Shift your weight onto the rear leg and turn the foot of the rear leg back. Turn on the ball of the rear foot. Raise the forward knee and keep your arms up.

The fighter on the left uses two hands to block his opponent's powerful roundhouse kick.

4

3

3. Kick in a semicircle, turning with your hip. Turning the hip increases the power of the kick. Keep your arms up for protection.

4. After the kick, pull your foot down as quickly as possible, returning to the fighting stance to protect your body.

SIDE KICK

The side kick is a very fast and powerful blow to the head or body. This kick should make contact with the heel or the side of the foot. The side kick gains much of its power from the twist of the hips that drives the foot into an opponent.

1. Stand in a fighting stance and focus on your opponent.

1

The kickboxer on the right tries to unbalance his opponent, who is attempting a side kick.

KICKING PRACTICE
Holding a partner's hand, perform a side kick, slowly, twenty times, without lowering the kicking foot. This practice exercise not only sharpens kicking technique, but also improves balance and coordination.

2. Bring the front knee up quickly and turn on the rear leg, pointing the heel of the kicking leg forward.

3. Kick in a straight line, turning the hip in the direction of the kick. The side of the foot or the heel should hit the opponent's body.

2

3

LOW KICK

The low kick is a circular move used to attack an opponent's shin or thigh. This kick often results in a knockout.

This well-executed and powerful low kick twists the opponent's leg to one side, pushing him off balance.

1

2

1. Starting in a fighting stance, step forward, slightly, putting your weight on your front leg. Begin turning your hips, rear leg, and rear arm forward.

2. Pivot on the rear foot, turning the thigh, hip, side of the body, and swinging arm forward, in a line. Push your swinging arm in a straight line toward your opponent's head. Use your rear arm for protection, holding up your hands as you kick.

The low kick should be used from the same distance as a punching technique.

It is important to thrust with the hip for the whole movement of a low kick.

1

2

BLOCK AND COUNTER

1. If an opponent attacks with a low kick, block the kick with your shin.

2. When the opponent lowers his or her foot after the low kick has been blocked, counter with a front kick to the body.

21

KNEE STRIKE

The knee strike is allowed only in Thai boxing, the toughest form of kickboxing. In Thai boxing, it is legal to use the knees and elbows to strike an opponent. Throws are also permitted.

The knee strike is a devastating technique. It can enable a small kickboxer to overcome a larger, stronger opponent.

Muay Thai *is a traditional form of kickboxing. Knee strikes, kicks, and throws win more points than punches in* Muay Thai.

KICKBOXING

1. Stand in the fighting stance.

2. Grab your opponent's head with both hands.

3. Pull his or her head down while pushing your knee up and your hip forward.

4. Return to the fighting stance.

PAD PRACTICE

Practice the knee strike at full power with a trainer who is using thai pads. A good trainer will be able to withstand blows from both knees, one after another, as well as punches, kicks, and elbow strikes. The trainer can move the pads to vary the speed of practice.

BACK KICK

The back kick is one of the most powerful kicks in any martial art, and it is often a knockout blow. This kick should be delivered in one swift movement, making contact with the heel.

1. Stand in a fighting stance and focus on your opponent.

Always make sure your partner is ready before throwing a back kick in practice.

The kickboxer in yellow lands a well-aimed back kick directly beneath his opponent's protecting arms.

2. Raise the heel of your forward leg while turning your head back, keeping your eyes on your target. Turn your body around, pivoting on your forward leg and pulling your other leg up to kick. You must turn around as quickly as possible.

3. Kick your raised leg straight back.

The kickboxer on the right connects with a perfect back kick, striking his opponent on the body, beneath his arms. The kicker uses the swinging motion of his arms to generate power. A back kick should be executed in one quick movement.

COUNTERING PUNCHES

In kickboxing, when your opponent throws a punch, it's not enough just to defend yourself. You should launch a counterattack at the same time.

You can counter a jab with a straight front kick. Before the jab hits you, shift your weight backward and kick at your opponent's body with your forward leg.

COUNTERING A JAB

1. Stand in a fighting stance.

2. As your opponent attacks with a jab, step away to the side and shift your weight onto your rear leg.

3. To start your counter, shift your weight back onto the front leg. At the same time, throw a punch to your opponent's head.

2

3

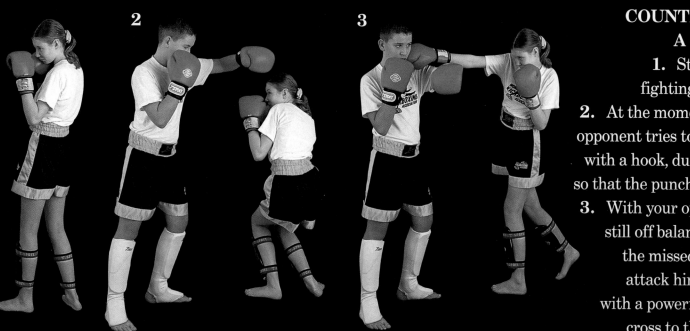

2

3

COUNTERING A HOOK

1. Stand in a fighting stance.

2. At the moment your opponent tries to hit you with a hook, duck down so that the punch misses.

3. With your opponent still off balance from the missed punch, attack him or her with a powerful right cross to the head.

COUNTERING KICKS

A kick is a powerful weapon. If you are defending against a kick, it is worth remembering that a kicker is slightly off balance after throwing a kick.

COUNTERING A SIDE KICK

1. Stand in a fighting stance.

2. As your opponent attacks with a side kick, take a step backward so that the kick misses.

3. While the attacker is lowering his or her foot from the missed kick, step forward and throw a right cross at his or her chin.

1

1   2

COUNTERING A FRONT KICK

1. Stand in a fighting stance.

2. As your opponent throws a front kick, step to the right to avoid the kick and turn your left arm down, blocking the kick with your left forearm.

2

3

COUNTERING A ROUNDHOUSE KICK

The roundhouse kick is a powerful technique, but it can be effectively countered. As your opponent tries to kick you with a left roundhouse to the body, step to the left and counterattack with a low kick to the leg on which your opponent is standing. This move should unbalance your opponent and give you the advantage.

3

3. Counterattack with a low kick to your opponent's forward leg.

USEFUL INFORMATION

Kickboxing Web sites give advice on getting started, training, techniques, and competitions.

International Kickboxing Federation (IKF)
www.ikfkickboxing.com

International Sport Karate Association (ISKA)
www.iska.com

Thai Boxing Association of the USA
www.thaiboxing.com

World Kickboxing and Karate Association (WKA)
www.wka.co.uk

Useful addresses:
International Kickboxing Federation
9385 Old State Highway
P.O. Box 1205
Newcastle, CA 95658
(916) 663-2467

International Sport Karate Association
P.O. Box 90147
Gainesville, FL 32607
(352) 331-0260

World Kickboxing and Karate Association
James Court, 63 Gravely Lane
Erdington, B23 6LX, UK
(011) 44 121 382 2995

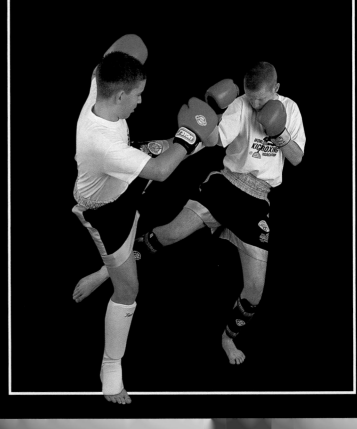

All the Internet addresses (URLs) given in this book were valid at the time of going to press. Due to the dynamic nature of the Internet, however, some addresses may have changed, or sites may have ceased to exist since publication. While the author and publishers regret any inconvenience to readers, they can accept no responsibility for any Internet changes.

KICKBOXING

KICKBOXING TERMS

back kick: a powerful kick executed by kicking backward in a straight line

blocking: using the arms, knees, or hands to stop an opponent's blows

dojo: training studio

fighting stance: the position from which kickboxers launch punches, kicks, and other blows, protecting the head with the shoulders and fists

front kick: a straightforward kick that makes contact with the ball of the kicking foot

hook: a sideways punch executed in a semicircular movement with the elbow pointing away from the body

jab: a short, sharp punch executed with the front hand, in which the front arm and hand extend forward from the body

knee strike: a blow struck with the knee to an opponent's body

knockout: a blow that leaves a kickboxer unable to get up within ten seconds

low kick: a kick to an opponent's thigh or shin that makes contact with the kicker's shin

right cross: a powerful punch executed with the rear right hand

roundhouse kick: a semicircular kick that strikes with the top of the foot or the shin

side kick: a powerful, straight kick executed from a stance in which the kicker faces the target sideways

Thai boxing: the toughest form of kickboxing, which allows elbow strikes and throws that are prohibited in semi-, light-, and full-contact kickboxing

thai pads: protective pads that are tied onto a trainer's forearms and serve as targets at which students can practice punches and kicks

uppercut: a powerful, upward punch, usually targeted at an opponent's chin

WKA: World Kickboxing and Karate Association, the world's largest and oldest kickboxing organization

INDEX

back kick 24–25
basics 8
boxing gloves 7

combat position 8
countering 26–29

fist 8
foot protectors 7
front kick 14–15,
  28–29

groin protector 7

head guard 7
history 6
hook 13, 27

jab 9, 26

karate 6
kicks 14–21, 24–25,
  28–29
kit 7
knee attack 22–23
knockout 10

Lewis, Joe 6
low kick 20–21

mouth guard 7

protection 7
punches 9–13, 26–27

right cross 10–11
roundhouse kick
  16–17, 29

safety equipment 7
shin guards 7
side kick 18–19, 28
skipping 7
stance 8
stretching 7

thai pads 11, 23

uppercut 12

warming up 7
World War II 6